Lovely HULL POTTERY Book 2

More of the Hull History

I now have well over 600 different pieces in my collection and have learned enough new facts to make this second volume on Hull pottery possible. It is hoped that this second volume will make the collecting of this fine ware even more interesting.

Most collectors are now aware of how everything was destroyed by flood and fire at the Hull pottery plant on June 16, 1950. This seems to enhance the desirability of collecting Hull, especially the pre-1950 lines. I have found that many are adding lines from the 1952-1960s to their collections, as well, and are paying rather high prices for these pieces.

I would like to add some more to the history found in my first book. Some of the information was found in an article in the "Pottery Collectors' Newsletter" by Norris Schneider a few years ago.

In 1862 Addis E. Hull was born at Deavertown, Ohio. He was from a large family of eleven children. His parents, the Henry Hulls, had imigrated from Ireland to this country.

In 1901 Mr. Hull was one of the organizers of the Globe Stoneware Company. In 1905, due to a disagreement, he and two other gentlemen left this company and formed the A. E. Hull Pottery Company. Mr. Hull was president, J. D. Young superintendent, and W. A. Watts was the secretary-treasurer.

In 1907 they bought the Acme China Company of Crooksville, Ohio and the Hull Company changed from the production of stoneware to kitchenware.

By the end of World War I they began importing some items, as it was cheaper than their own cost of production. This period was between 1921-1929.

1927-1932 was the period of tile manufacturing for the company, but the depression years brought many problems to the company. Mr. Hull died in 1930. The price of tile was selling for below production costs. The oldest son, Addis E. Hull Jr., took over the company and established it in the field of art pottery. In 1937 he left to manage the Shawnee Pottery Company. During the same year the company aided the economy of Crooksville by employing 450 workers to make a special order of eleven million pieces for the Shulton Company in New York. W. A. Watt's son, Gerald Watts, took over as president until the disaster of the flood and fire.

Mr. James Brannon Hull became president at that time. He reorganized the company and it was opened at the beginning of 1952. Today they are producing casual serving ware and a line for florists.

Price Guide To Accompany

Lovely Hull Pottery

Volume II

$1.50

by

SHARON LORAINE FELKER

Published in the United States of America by
WALLACE-HOMESTEAD BOOK COMPANY
1912 Grand Ave., Des Moines, Iowa 50305

ISBN: 0-87069-209-7

Again I must state that the prices shown are only an average. In some areas prices are much higher than in other areas.

PLATE 1

Top row: 1. $12-$15; 2. $12-$15; 3. $20-$25; 4. $15-$20.

Middle row: 1. $15-$20; 2. & 4. $12-$15, the pair; 3. $12-$15; 5. $12-$15.

Bottom row: 1. $12-$15; 2. $5-$7.50; 3. $25-$30; 4. $5-$7.50; 5. $12-$15.

PLATE 2

Top row: 1. $25-$35; 2. $12-$15; 3. $20-$25; 4. $12-$15.

Middle row: 1. $10-$12; 2. $12-$15; 3. $18-$20; 4. $10-$12; 5. $10-$12.

Bottom row: 1. $10-$12; 2. $15-$18; 3. or 4. $10-$12; 5. or 6. $10-$12; 7. $10-$12.

PLATE 3

Top row: 1. $12-$15; 2. $7.50-$12; 3. $12-$15; 4. $12-$15; 5. $12-$18.

Middle row: 1. $12-$18; 2. $7.50-$12; 3. $15-$18; 4. $25-$35.

Bottom row: 1. $12-$15; 2. or 3. $20-$25; 4. $12-$15.

PLATE 4

Top row: 1. $12-$15; 2 & 4. $12-$15, the pair; 3. $15-$20; 5. $25-$35.

Middle row: 1. $12-$15; 2. $15-$25; 3. $15-$25; 4. $5-$7.50; 5. $25-$30; 6. $5-$7.50.

Bottom row: 1. $12-$15; 2. $12-$15; 3. $15-$18; 4. $12-$15; 5. $12-$15.

PLATE 5

Top row: 1. $12-$18; 2. $12-$18; 3. $18-$25; 4. $12-$15; 5. $12-$15; 6. $12-$15.

Middle row: 1. $12-$15; 2. $12-$15; 3. $12-$15; 4. $12-$15; 5. $12-$15.

Bottom row: 1. $12-$18; 2. $12-$18; 3. $50-$75; 4. $50-$75; 5. $12-$15.

PLATE 6

Top row: 1. $15-$20; 2. $15-$20; 3. $12-$15; 4. $10-$12; 5. $12-$15.

Middle row: 1. $12-$15; 2. $15-$20; 3. $15-$20; 4. with lid, $25-$30; 5. $12-$15.

Bottom row: 1. $15-$20; 2. $5-$7.50; 3. $5-$10; 4. $5-$10; 5. $5-$10.

PLATE 7

Top row: 1. $5-$10; 2. $5-$7.50; 3. $5-$10; 4. $5-$10; 5. $5-$10.

Middle row: 1. $5-$7.50; 2. $5-$7.50; 3. $7.50-$12; 4. $10-$12; 5. $7.50-$12.

Bottom row: 1. $10-$15; 2. $5-$7.50; 3. $7.50-$10; 4. $7.50-$10; 5. $10-$15.

PLATE 8

Top row: 1. $12-$18; 2. & 4. $15-$18, the pair; 3. $15-$20; 5. $12-$15.

Middle row: 1. $12-$18; 2. $15-$20; 3. $12-$15; 4. $20-$25; 5. $20-$25.

Bottom row: 1. $12-$15; 2. $12-$15; 3. $12-$15; 4. $12-$18.

PLATE 9

Top row: 1. $5-$7.50; 2. $5-$7.50; 3. $30-$45; 4. $5-$7.50 5. $25-$30.

Middle row: 1. $12-$15; 2. $12-$15; 3. $12-$15; 4. $25-$35; 5. $15-$18.

Bottom row: 1. $10-$15; 2. $8-$12; 3. $5-$7.50; 4. $12-$15; 5. $8-$12.

PLATE 10

Top row: 1. $30-$45; 2. $5-$7.50; 3. $15-$18; 4. $5-$7.50; 5. $25-$30.

Middle row: 1. $12-$18; 2. $25-$35; 3. $30-$45; 4. $10-$12.50; 5. $10-$12.50.

Bottom row: 1. $12-$15; 2. $10-$12.50; 3. $25-$30; 4. $15-$20; 5. $20-$25.

PLATE 11

Top row: 1. $25-$30; 2. $5-$7.50; 3. $5-$7.50; 4. $5-$7.50; 5. $10-$12.50; 6. $10-$12.50.

Middle row: 1. $15-$20; 2. $12-$15; 3. $12-$15; 4. $5-$7.50; 5. $5-$7.50; 6. $12-$18.

Bottom row: 1. $8-$10; 2. $10-$12; 3. $20-$25; 4. $10-$15; 5. $7.50-$10; 6. $35-$45; 7. $20-$25.

PLATE 12

Top row: 1. $10-$12; 2. $10-$15; 3. $10-$15; 4. $10-$15; 5. $10-$15.

Middle row: 1. $8-$10; 2. $10-$15; 3. $5-$7.50; 4. $10-$15; 5. $8-$12.

Bottom row: 1. $12-$15; 2. $8-$12; 3. $8-$12; 4. $10-$15; 5. $8-$12.

PLATE 13

Top row: 1. $3-$4; 2. $7-$10; 3. $3-$4; 4. $12-$15; 5. $8-$12; 6. $12-$15.

Middle row: 1. $25-$30 for the complete set.

Bottom row: 1.-3. $12-$18 for the set; 4. $25-$35; 5. $15-$18.

PLATE 14

Top row: 1. $8-$12; 2. $8-$12; 3. $8-$12; 4. $5-$7.50; 5. $5-$7.50.

Middle row: 1. $10-$12; 2. $5-$7.50; 3. $10-$15; 4. $5-$7.50; 5. $10-$12.

Bottom row: 1. $10-$12; 2. $8-$12; 3. $8-$12; 4. $7.50-$10; 5. $5-$10.

PLATE 15

Top row: 1. $25-$35; 2. & 4. $10-$15, the pair; 3. $25-$35; 5. $25-$35.

Middle row: 1. $7.50-$10; 2. $25-$30; 3. $7.50-$10; 4. & 6. $8-$12, the pair; 5. $10-$15, with spoon.

Bottom row: 1. $15-$20; 2. $15-$20; 3. $7.50-$10; 4. $25-$30; 5. $7.50-$10.

PLATE 16

Top row: 1. $12-$18; 2. $12-$15; 3. $12-$15; 4. $12-$15; 5. $15-$20.

Middle row: 1. $15-$20; 2. $12-$15; 3. $12-$15; 4. $5-$7.50; 5. $5-$7.50

Bottom row: 1. $12-$18; 2. $12-$15; 3. $15-$20; 4. $12-$15.

PLATE 17

Top row: 1. $12-$15; 2. $10-$12; 3. $12-$15; 4. $15-$20.

Middle row: 1. $10-$15; 2. $15-$20; 3. $12-$18; 4. $12-$18.

Bottom row: 1. $12-$15; 2. $5-$7.50; 3. $12-$18; 4. $5-$7.50 5. $10-$15.

PLATE 18

Top row: 1. $50-$75; 2. $12-$15; 3. $5-$7.50; 4. $5-$7.50; 5. $25-$30; 6. $5-$7.50.

Middle row: 1. $10-$12; 2. $10-$12; 3. $12-$15; 4. $10-$12; 5. $10-$15.

Bottom row: 1. $10-$12; 2. $7.50-$10; 3. $8-$12; 4. $8-$12.

PLATE 19

Top row: 1. $15-$18; 2. $12-$15; 3. $12-$15; 4. $12-$15; 5. $12-$15.

Middle row: 1. $12-$15; 2. $12-$15; 3. $15-$20; 4. $8-$12; 5. $12-$15.

Bottom row: 1. $10-$15; 2. $10-$15; 3. $12-$15; 4. $12-$15; 5. $12-$15.

PLATE 20

Top row: 1. $12-$15; 2. $12-$15; 3. $25-$35; 4. $12-$18; $12-$18.

Middle row: 1. $10-$12; 2. $12-$15; 3. $10-$12; 4. $15-$25; 5. $5-$7.50.

Bottom row: 1. $5-$7.50; 2. $10-$15; 3. $10-$15; 4. $10-$15; 5. $12-$18; 6. $10-$15.

PLATE 21

Top row: 1. $15-$20; 2. $12-$18; 3. $12-$18; 4. $10-$12.

Middle row: 1. $12-$15; 2. $12-$15; 3. $5-$7.50; 4. $25-$30; 5. $5-$7.50; 6. $12-$15.

Bottom row: 1. $12-$15; 2. $12-$15; 3. $5-$7.50; 4. $12-$18; 5. $5-$7.50; 6. $15-$25.

PLATE 22

Top row: 1. $12-$15; 2. $8-$12; 3. $8-$12; 4. $8-$12; 5. $8-$12.

Middle row: 1. $8-$12; 2. $8-$12; 3. $8-$12; 4. $12-$15.

Bottom row: 1. $15-$20; 2. $8-$12; 3. $8-$12; 4. $8-$12; 5. $8-$12; 6. $8-$12.

PLATE 23

Top row: This set is difficult to put a price on as I have seen no others with which to compare it. It is worth whatever someone is willing to pay. I paid $125 for the set, and one mug has a chip on it.

Middle row: 1. $18-$30; 2. $18-$30; 3. $18-$30; 4. $18-$30; 5. $12-$15.

Bottom row: 1. $15-$20; 2. $12-$15; 3. $10-$15; 4. $10-$15.

Some of the pieces are not marked Hull. Some are marked U.S.A. with a number series. Others have patent numbers and there are still others with no mark at all. The Thistle design lacks the Hull mark. The 1940-41 Blackwell Wielandy Company catalog reprinted by Antiques Research Publications shows "3 vases in the Thistle Pattern in assorted shapes in two toned pastel blue or pink colors, raised floral and leaf design in pink, blue and green colors. Average height 6½". One dozen assorted, 3 kinds in 2 colors sold for $8 per dozen." In this catalog is also shown the Colonial girl planter with basket. I have three of these. One is white glossy glaze with blue trim, impressed Hull Art U.S.A. 954; another is marked the same with pink glossy glaze and blue trim; the third is white matte glaze with orange trim and is marked U.S.A. 954, only. The ad states "Satin finish pottery, in ivory color, decorated with blue, yellow, or red hat and sash. Height 7¾". 1 dozen assorted colors to the carton. Per dozen $14.40."

A bit more expensive were the Hull pottery Orchid design flower vases. "Per dozen pieces $20.40. Two styles, beautiful matte finish in shaded and tinted colors of pink, blue, and ivory: decorated in raised orchid motif in harmonizing colors. One style in semi-fan shape: other style in graceful handled shape. Height 8½". Packed in matching pairs. One dozen pieces in carton."

Two other pieces are shown and one is the Peasant Girl Head planter. "Four colors, Hull Pottery, lustre finish in pastel blue, pink, or yellow colors, and matte finish ivory. Height 5½", 1 dozen assorted, 4 colors to the carton. Per dozen $9.60." The last piece shown is a Horn Of Plenty. It is pictured in my first book; plate 20, bottom row, No. 1. It came in ". . . four colors, lustre finish in pastel pink, blue, and yellow, and matte finish ivory. Height 5½", 1 dozen assorted 4 colors in carton. Per dozen $9.60."

I would like to take this opportunity to correct a mistake in my first book. On the bottom row of plate 22, numbers 4 and 5, a pair of Oriental figurines, are not Hull but Shawnee pottery. My apologies for misleading anyone on this. Please remember there were "Hulls" connected with the Shawnee company.

Designs Produced from the New Plant

Blossom Flight	1955
Woodland, high gloss	1952
Capri (green, coral)	1961
Tropicana	1950s
Tokay	1958
Serenade (pink, blue, yellow)	1957
Ebb Tide	1954
Continental (blue, persimmon, green)	1959
Butterfly and Blossoms	1956

Sun Glow is another line mentioned by Mr. Hull, but I have not been able to identify this line.

In Volume 1, #3 of the "Hull Collectors' Newsletter", Ms. Marge Wheeler came up with some information about the dinnerware "House 'n Garden" line. It came in four colors, orange, forest green, yellow-tan, and the mirror brown glaze that is now being made. This ware is not always marked Hull, but is sometimes marked ovenproof (script). The other colors were discontinued about ten years ago. Mr. R. E. Smith has pieces of dinnerware in a turquoise color that are similar in shape but are marked hull u.s.a. Crestone (script) © OVEN-PROOF.

Pre-1950 Lines

Red Riding Hood	1937-47	Dogwood	?
Jack-in-the-Pulpit	?	Woodland (matte)	?
Magnolia	1947		
Orchid	1940-41	Thistle	1940-41
Narcissus	?	Bow Knot	1949
Tulip	1940-41	Wild Flower	?
Camellia	?	Waterlily	?
Poppy	?	Parchment and Pine	?

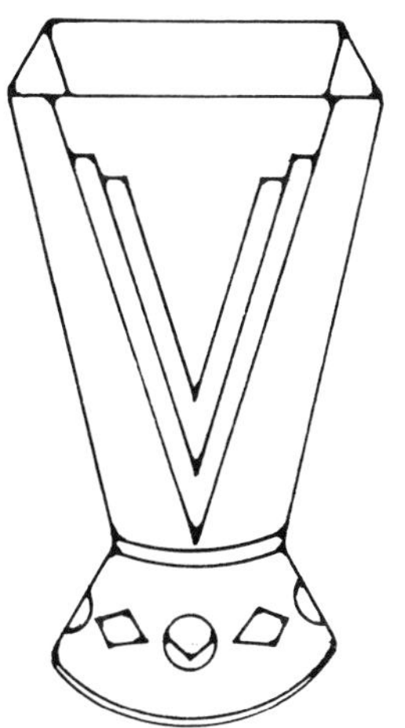

Mrs. Fred Pevott owns the illustrated Apostles' pitcher on the top. The pitcher is 9¼" to the tip of the handle. The base diameter is 4-3/8". There is no glaze on the inside of the base. It is marked Hull (script), only. It is in two shades of blue, a powder blue and a dusty shade of blue. It is clear glazed and has a high gloss.

The vase on the bottom is owned by Norman Haas, Jackson, Mississippi. It is 7" high, the base diameter is 3¾" while the square top measures 3¾". The outer edges are lavender. The double "v" is green with pink inside the "v." The interior of the vase is pink. The piece is unmarked, but bears a paper Hull label. It has a matte finish.

Plate 1

Bow Knot Design, 1949

These pieces are matte finished and marked with Hull Art U.S.A. in raised letters. I want to list the known pieces and will indicate when that piece is shown. I will leave space for you to pencil in the missing pieces that I'm sure do exist. (* means the item is pictured.) In an article awhile ago, it was stated that the Hull Company paid an internationally known artist $3,000 for 30 approved pencil sketches featuring the Bow Knot design.

Pitcher, B-1-5½"
*Vase, B-2-5"
Vase, B-3-6½"
*Vase, B-4-6½"
*Cornucopia, B-5-7½"
Planter, B-6-6½"
*Vase, B-7-8½"
*Vase B-8-8½"
*Vase, B-9-8½"
*Vase, B-10-10½"
Vase, B-11-10½"
*Basket, B-12-10½"
Double cornucopia, B-13-13"
*Console bowl, B-16-13½"
*Candleholders, B-17-3½"
*Bowl, B-18-5¾"
*Jardiniere, B-19-9 3/8"
*Teapot, B-20-6"
*Creamer, B-21-4"
*Covered sugar, B-22-4"

Cup and saucer wall vase, B-24-6"
Basket, B-25-6½"
Pitcher wall vase, B-26-6"
Whisk broom wall vase, B-27-8"
Plate or plaque, B-28-10"
Basket, B-29-12"

Top row: 1. Vase, B-8-8½". 2. Vase, B-9-8½". 3. Jardiniere, B-19-9 3/8". 4. Vase, B-10-10½".
Middle row: 1. Vase, B-10-10½". 2. Candleholder, B-17-3½". 3. Cornucopia, B-5-7½". 4. Candleholder, B-17-3½". 5. Vase, B-7-8½".
Bottom row: 1. Bowl, B-18-5¾". 2. Covered sugar, B-22-4". 3. Teapot, B-20-6". 4. Creamer, B-21-4". 5. Vase, B-4-6½".

Plate 2

BOW KNOT DESIGN (continued)

Top row: 1. Basket, B-12-10½". 2. Vase, B-8-8½". 3. Console bowl, B-16-13½". 4. Vase, B-2-5".

Tulip Design, 1940-41

All pieces are of the matte finish and have impressed marks and block letters, HULL U.S.A.

Middle row: 1. Vase, 100-33-6½". 2. Vase, 1-?-33-7". 3. Jardiniere, can't read the mark. 4. Vase, 107-33-6". 5. Vase, 108-33-6".

Bottom row: 1. Vase, 102-33-6". 2. Vase, 100-33-10". 3. and 4. Bud vases, 1 ?-33-6". 5. Vase, 117-33-5". 6. Vase, 117-33-5". 7. Vase, 106-33-6".

Known pieces in the Tulip design:

*Vase, 100-33-6½"
*Vase, 100-33-10"

*Basket, 102-33-6"

Vase, 105-33-8"
*Vase, 106-33-6"
*Vase, 107-33-6"
*Vase, 108-33-6"

Vase, 110-33-6"
Vase, 111-33-6"

Planter, 116-33-6"
*Vase, 117-33-5"

Plate 3

Wild Flower Design

These pieces have a matte finish and are marked Hull Art U.S.A. in raised letters.

Top row: 1. Vase, 75-8½". 2. Pitcher, W-2-5½". 3. Vase, 53-8½". 4. Vase, W-9-8½". 5. Vase, W-12-9½".

Middle row: 1. Vase, W-13-9½". 2. Pitcher vase, W-2-5½". 3. Pitcher vase, W-11-8½". 4. Vase, W-18-12½".

Here is a puzzle that hasn't been solved yet. I have three vases (and know of several others) that have the Wild Flower design, but a different set of markings. Could it be that they were produced during different periods?

Known pieces in the Wild Flower design:

Vase, W-1-5½"
*Pitcher, W-2-5½"
Vase, W-3-5½"
Vase, W-4-6½"
Vase, W-5-6½"
Vase, W-6-7½"
Cornucopia, W-7-7½"
Vase, W-8-7½"
*Vase, W-9-8½"
Cornucopia, W-10-8½"
*Pitcher, W-11-8½"
*Vase, W-12-9½"

*Vase, W-13-9½"
Vase, W-14-10½"
Vase, W-15-10½"
Basket, W-16-10½"
Urn, W-17-12½"
*Vase, W-18-12½"

Vase, W-20-15½"
Console bowl, W-21-12"
Candleholders, no mark
*Vase, 53-8½"
*Vase, 75-8½"
Vase, 52-5¼"

Water Lily Design

These pieces are of the matte finish and have a raised mark, Hull Art U.S.A.

Bottom row: 1. Vase, L-6-6½". 2. and 3. Double cornucopias, L-27-12". 4. Cornucopia, L-7-6½".

Plate 4

WATER LILY DESIGN (continued)

Top row: 1. Vase, L-5-6½". 2. and 3. Candleholders, L-22. 3. Console bowl, L-21-13½". 5. Basket, L-14-10½".

Middle row: 1. Vase, L-8-8½". 2. and 3. Vases, L-12-10½". 4. Creamer, glossy glaze, L-19-5". 5. Teapot, L-18-6". 6. Creamer, L-19-5".

Bottom row: 1. Cornucopia, L-7-6½". 2. Bowl, L-23-5½". 3. Vase, L-11-9½". 4. Vase, L-2-5½". 5. Vase, L-A-8½".

The following pieces are known in the Water Lily design:

Vase, L-1-5½"
*Vase, L-2-5½"
Pitcher, L-3-5½"
Vase, L-4-6½"
*Vase, L-5-6½"
*Vase, L-6-6½"
*Cornucopia, L-7-6½"
*Vase, L-8-8½"
Vase, L-9-8½"
Vase, L-10-9½"
*Vase, L-11-9½"
*Vase, L-12-10½"
Urn, L-13-10½"

*Basket, L-14-10½"

*Teapot, L-18-6"
*Creamer, L-19-5"

*Console bowl, L-21-13½"
*Candleholders, L-22
Bowl, L-23-5½"
Jardiniere, L-24-8½"

*Double cornucopia, L-27-12"
*Vase, L-A-8½"

Plate 5

Rosella Design

This pattern has a glossy glaze and is marked Hull Art in raised letters.

Top row: 1. Ewer, R-11-7"L. 2. Ewer, R-11-7"R. 3. Basket, R-12-7". 4. Vase, R-8-6½". 5. Wall vase, R-10-6¼". 6. Vase, R-1-5".

Middle row: 1. and 2. Vases, R-15-8½". 3. Cornucopia, R-13-8½"R. 4. Vase, R-5-6½". 5. Vase, R-7-6½".

Bottom row: 1. Ewer, R-9-6½"L. 2. Ewer, R-9-6½"R. 3. and 4. Pair of lamps, no mark. 5. Vase, R-14-8½".

The following items are known in this pattern:

*Vase, R-1-5"
Vase, R-2-5"
Sugar, R-3-5½"
Creamer, R-4-5½"
*Vase, R-5-6½"
Vase, R-6-6½"
*Vase, R-7-6½"
*Vase, R-8-6½"
*Ewer, R-9-6½"L
*Ewer, R-9-6½"R
*Wall vase, R-10-6¼"
*Ewer, R-11-7"L
*Ewer, R-11-7"R
*Basket, R-12-7"
Cornucopia, R-13-8½"L
*Cornucopia, R-13-8½"R
*Vase, R-14-8½"
*Vase, R-15-8½"
*Lamps, no mark

Mr. J. B. Hull said there were no lamps made for the regular market, and that the lamps that we have were probably made by employees on their own time for their own use or for gifts. This may explain why there are so few to be found.

One occasionally runs across an advertising plaque. These were used in stores for their displays. These also are hard to find and command good prices.

Plate 6

Dogwood (Wildrose) Design

These pieces are matte finished and their mark is impressed HULL U.S.A. block letters.

Top row: 1. Vase, 502-6½". 2. Basket, 501-7½". 3. Vase, 509-6½". 4. Bowl, 514-4". 5. Vase, 513-6½".

Middle row: 1. Vase, 513-6½". 2. Vase, 502-6½". 3. Pitcher, 505-6½". 4. This was sold to me as a watering can, but it could be the teapot of this line minus the lid, 507-6½". 5. Vase, 504-8½".

Bottom row: 1. Vase, 510-10½". 2. Candleholder, 512. 3. Miscellaneous dish, it resembles the Tokay line, but is not marked such. It is impressed (script) Hull U.S.A. 19. 4. Vase, impressed (script) Hull U.S.A. 37. 5. Vase, impressed (script) Hull U.S.A. 71.

The following items are known in the Dogwood design:

*Basket, 501-7½"
*Vase, 502-6½"
Vase, 503-8½"
*Vase, 504-8½"
*Pitcher, 505-6½"

*"Teapot" 507-6½"
Vase, 508-10½"
*Vase, 509-6½"
*Vase, 510-10½"
Cornucopia, 511-11½"
*Candleholder, 512

*Vase, 513-6½"
*Bowl, 514-4"
Vase, 515-8½"
Vase, 516-4¾"
Vase, 517-4¾"

Ewer, 520-4¾"
Bowl, 521-7"
Cornucopia, 522-4"

Plate 7

Planters and Vases

All of these items have the mark of Hull (script) U.S.A. They were probably produced in the 1950s.

Top row: 1. Three-bowl planter, 107. 2. Vase, 42. 3. Planter, 403. 4. Planter, 82. 5. Vase, 102.

Middle row: 1. Planter, 31. 2. Vase, impressed 100 U.S.A., only. 3. Planter, a Tokay shape but not the glaze and color and not marked Tokay, 5. 4. Cornucopia, similar to Tokay but not listed as such, 49. 5. Bucket planter, 94B-5".

Bottom row: 1. Vase, 111. 2. Planter, 121. 3. Planter, 19. 4. Urn-vase, impressed URN-VASE HULL U.S.A. (block letters) 419, and may have been before the 1950 period. 5. Vase, 108.

Plate 8

Camellia (Open Rose) Design

Matte glazed with raised block letters, HULL U.S.A.

Top row: 1. Vase, 103-8½". 2. and 4. Bird candleholders, 117-6½". 3. Console bowl, 116-12". 5. Vase, 129-7".
Middle row: 1. Vase, 108-8½". 2. Basket, 107-8". 3. Vase, 120-6¼". 4. Hand vase, 126-8½". 5. Lamp vase, 139-10½".
Bottom row: 1. and 2. Cornucopias, 101-8½". 3. Vase, 102-8½". 4. Vase, 143-8½".

Items known in the Camellia line:

*Cornucopia, 101-8½"
*Vase, 102-8½"
*Vase, 103-8½"

Vase, 105-7"
*Pitcher, 106-13¼"
*Basket, 107-8"
*Vase, 108-8½"
*Teapot, 110-8½"
*Creamer, 111-5"
*Sugar, 112-5"
Vase, 113-6¼"
Urn, 114-8¼"
Vase, 115-6¼"
*Console bowl, 116-12"
*Candleholder, 117-6½"
Swan planter, 118-6½"
Vase, 119-8½"
*Vase, 120-6¼"
Vase, 121-6¼"
Vase, 122-6¼"

Vase, 123-6½"
Vase, 124-12"
Wall vase, 125-8½"
*Vase, 126-8½"
Vase, 127-4¾"
Pitcher, 128-4¾"
*Vase, 129-7"
Vase, 130-4¾"
Vase, 131-4¾"

Vase, 133-6¼"
Vase, 134-6¼"
Vase, 135-6¼"
Vase, 136-6¼"
Vase, 137-6¼"
Vase, 138-6¼"
*Lamp vase, 139-10½"

Vase, 141-8½"
Basket, 142-?
*Vase, 143-8½"

Plate 9

CAMELLIA (OPEN ROSE) DESIGN (continued)

Top row: 1. Sugar 112-5". 2. Creamer, 111-5". 3. Pitcher vase, 106-13¼". 4. Creamer, 111-5". 5. Teapot, 110-8½".

Poppy Design

These pieces have a matte finish with a raised mark HULL U.S.A. in block letters. This line seems to be rather scarce.

Middle row: 1. Bowl, 608-4¾". 2. Vase, 607-6½". 3. Vase, 611-6½". 4. Basket, 601-12". 5. Vase, 606-8½".

Planters

The following are impressed Hull (script) U.S.A.

Bottom row: 1. Large swan, 69. 2. Medium swan, 80. 3. Small swan, no mark. 4. Rooster planter, 54. 5. Medium duck, 75.

Known pieces in the Poppy line:

*Basket, 601-12"
Vase, 602-?

Vase, 605-8½"
*Vase, 606-8½"
*Vase, 607-6½"
Vase, 607-10½"
*Bowl, 608-4¾"

Vase, 610-13½"
*Vase, 611-6½"
Vase, 612-6¼"

Plate 10

Magnolia Design, 1947

There are two different types of the Magnolia design. One has the matte finish while the other has a glossy finish. The matte pieces are marked in a number series and are from the middle 40s. The glossy glazed pieces are marked with an H and number series. It is uncertain if they were produced at the same time. They are both marked in raised letters, Hull Art U.S.A.

Top row: 1. Pitcher vase, 18-13½". 2. and 4. Candleholders, 27-4". 3. Vase, 1-8½". 5. Teapot, 23-6½".

Middle row: 1. Pitcher, 5-7". 2. Basket, 10-10½". 3. Vase, 17-12¼". 4. Vase, H-7-6½". 5. Pitcher, H-3-5½".

Bottom row: 1. Vase, H-9-8½". 2. Vase, H-6-6½". 3. Vase, H-18-12½". 4. Vase, H-12-10½". 5. Double cornucopia, H-15-12".

Known matte Magnolia pieces:

*Vase, 1-8½"
Vase, 2-8½"
Vase, 3-8½"
Vase, 4-6¼"
*Pitcher, 5-7"
Double cornucopia, 6-12"
Vase, 7-8½"
Vase, 8-10½"
Vase, 9-10½"
*Basket, 10-10½"
Vase, 11-6¼"
Vase, 12-6¼"
Vase, 13-4¾"
Pitcher, 14-4¾"

Vase, 15-6¼"

*Vase, 17-12¼"
*Pitcher, 18-13½"
Cornucopia, 19-8½"
Vase, 20-15"

Vase, 22-12½"
*Teapot, 23-6½"
Creamer, 24-3¾"
Sugar, 25-3¾"
Console bowl, 26-12½"
*Candleholder, 27-4"

Plate 11

MAGNOLIA DESIGN, 1947 (continued)

Known pieces in the glossy Magnolia design:

*Vase, H-1-5½"
Vase, H-2-5½"
*Pitcher, H-3-5½"
Vase, H-4-6½"

*Vase, H-6-6½"
*Vase, H-7-6½"

*Vase, H-9-8½"
*Cornucopia, H-10-8½"

*Vase, H-12-10½"

*Vase, H-13-10½"

*Double cornucopia, H-15-12"

*Vase, H-18-12½"

*Teapot, H-20-6½"
*Creamer, H-21-3¾"
*Covered sugar, H-22-3¾"
*Console bowl, H-23-13"
*Candleholder, H-24

Top row: 1. Teapot, H-20-6½". 2. Covered sugar, H-22-3¾". 3. Creamer, H-21-3¾". 4. Vase, H-6-6½". 5. Vase, H-1-5½". 6. Vase, H-7-6½".

Middle row: 1. Vase, H-13-10½". 2. and 3. Cornucopias, H-10-8½". 4. and 6. Candleholders, H-24. 5. Console bowl, H-23-13".

The Tokay design was produced in 1958, impressed Tokay (script) U.S.A. and has a glossy glaze. The Jack-in-the-Pulpit design is a matte finish, impressed U.S.A. with a number series only. I have only two pieces of this line and it seems to be rather scarce.

Bottom row: 1. Planter, 9. 2. Cornucopia, 10. 3. Basket, 15. 4. Vase, 12. 5. Pitcher vase, 3. 6. Pitcher vase, 506-10". It also has a paper label stating it was a sample of the A. E. Hull Pottery Company. 7. Vase, 550/33-7½".

Items in the Tokay line:

Cornucopia, 1
Vase, 2
*Pitcher vase, 3
Vase, 4-8¼"
Urn planter, 5
Basket, 6

Bowl, 7
Vase, 8-10"
*Planter, 9 or, with cover, candy dish
Cornucopia, 10
Round basket, 11

*Vase, 12-12"
Pitcher vase, 13-12"
Console bowl, 14
*Basket, 15
Teapot, 16
Creamer, 17
Covered sugar, 18

Plate 12

Figural Planters and Vases

Most of these items are marked with an impressed Hull (script) U.S.A. Those that are different will be noted.

Top row: 1. Swan planter, 413. 2. Flying goose planter, 96. 3. Giraffe planter, 115. 4. Colonial girl planter, 954 U.S.A. There is no Hull mark on this one. 5. Colonial girl planter, impressed Hull Art U.S.A. 954. Both 4. and 5. were produced in 1940-41.

Middle row: 1. Poodle planter, 114. 2. Peasant girl head planter, impressed block letters HULL U.S.A. 204, 1940-41. 3. Small white swan, no mark. 4. Large swan planter, 23. 5. Medium-sized swan planter, 80.

Bottom row: 1. Rooster planter, impressed block letters HULL U.S.A., 951. 2. Double goose planter, 95. 3. Same as 2. 4. Same as middle row, No. 2. 5. Poodle head planter, © '55, 38.

Plate 13

Kitchen Items

Top row: 1. and 3. Salt and pepper shakers, impressed U.S.A. 44 only. 2. Grease jar, impressed Hull (script) U.S.A. NO. 43. 4. Cookie jar, impressed script Hull U.S.A. NO.-48. 5. Milk pitcher, impressed block letters HULL U.S.A. B-7-1pt. 6. Casserole, impressed Hull (script) U.S.A. B-2.

Middle row: 1.-6. Set of bowls, 1943 (?), the largest is marked with impressed block letters HULL U.S.A. B-19. The smallest has HULL U.S.A. B-14 impressed. The other bowls have no marks but have seals stating they were both ovenproof and coldproof.

Bottom row: 1.-3. These three bowls are impressed Hull (script) OVEN-PROOF U.S.A. The largest is marked B-1-9", the middle one B-1-7", and the small one B-1-5". 4. Duck cookie jar, impressed Hull (script) U.S.A. 966. 5. Cookie jar, impressed Hull (script) U.S.A. 0-8.

Plate 14

Ebb Tide Design, 1954

Ebb Tide has a glossy glaze and is impressed Hull (script) U.S.A. I have found that some of the pieces were not marked.

Top row: 1. Twin fish vase, no mark, should be E-2. 2. and 3. Fish vases, E-6. 4. Creamer, E-15. 5. Covered sugar, E-16.
Middle row: 1. and 5. Large double fish vases, E-9. 2. and 4. Candleholders, E-13. 3. Console bowl, E-12.
Bottom row: 1. Mermaid planter, no mark, should be E-3. 2. and 3. Double bud vases, impressed Hull (script) U.S.A. 103. 4. Dish or planter, impressed Hull (script) U.S.A. 34. 5. Planter, impressed (script) U.S.A. F3.

Known pieces of the Ebb Tide line:

Bud vase, E-1
*Vase, E-2-7"
*Mermaid planter, E-3
Pitcher vase, E-4
Basket, E-5
*Fish vase, E-6
Vase, E-7-11"
Mermaid ashtray, E-8
*Large double fish vase, E-9
Pitcher, E-10-14"
Large shell basket, E-11
*Console bowl, E-12
*Candleholder, E-13
Teapot, E-14
*Creamer, E-15
*Covered sugar, E-16

Plate 15

Little Red Riding Hood Design, 1937-47

According to Mr. J. B. Hull these pieces were blanks made by the Hull Pottery Company and sent to the Royal China and Novelty Company of Chicago, Illinois. The actual patent for this design was issued, June 29, 1943. Those pieces marked "patent applied for" would be the earliest ones of this line.

Pieces known in this design:

Butter dish
Match holder
String holder
Money bank
8" Pitcher
Large salt and pepper shakers
6-piece spice set

Covered jam or grease jar
8¼" Covered jar
Cannisters (coffee, tea)
Mustard pot with matching pottery spoon
Wall plaque
6½" Pitcher
Small creamer

Small sugar
Cookie jar
Large creamer
Large sugar
Teapot
Small salt and pepper shakers

There may be other items as well, as there are no records on this design known.

Top row: 1. Cookie jar, impressed Pat. Des-No. 135889, 967. 2. and 4. Salt and peppers, impressed Pat. Des-No 135889. 3. and 5. Cookie jars, impressed in script, Hull Ware, patent applied for, 967.

Middle row: 1. Creamer, Pat. Des-No 135889 impressed. 2. Teapot, U.S.A. only. 3. Sugar, impressed Pat. Des-NO 135889. 4. and 6. Small salt and peppers, no mark. 5. Mustard pot with matching pottery spoon, no mark.

Bottom row: 1. 8" pitcher, no mark. Parchment and Pine design. 2. Vase, S-1. 3. and 5. Candleholders, no mark, should be S-10. 4. Vase, S-4.

The Parchment and Pine pieces have a glossy glaze and are impressed in script Hull U.S.A. It is uncertain as to when this line was produced, but most agree it is from the new factory in the 1950s. The following pieces are known; not all were marked.

*Vase, S-1
Cornucopias, S-2-R, S-2-L
Basket, S-3
*Vase, S-4

Planter, S-5
Cornucopias, S-6-L, S-6-R
Pitcher vase, S-7
Basket, S-8

Console bowl, S-9
*Candleholder, S-10
Teapot, S-11
Creamer, S-12
Covered sugar, S-13

Plate 16

Serenade Design, 1957

These pieces have a textured finish, impressed in script Hull U.S.A. © '57. Each piece came in either of three colors, yellow, blue, or pink.

Top row: 1. Vase, S-12. 2. Planter, S-4. 3. and 4. Vases, S-6. 5. Pitcher, S-21.

Middle row: 1. Ashtray, S-23. 2. Vase, S-11. 3. Vase, S-1. 4. Creamer, S-18. 5. Covered sugar, S-19.

Bottom row: 1. Covered candy dish, S-3. 2. Planter, S-4. 3. Miscellaneous cookie jar, impressed Hull (script) U.S.A. O-18. 4. Pig planter, hand-painted flowers, impressed U.S.A. #60 only.

Known pieces in the Serenade design:

*Bud vase, S-1
Pitcher vase, S-2
*Urn, S-3 or, with lid, a candy dish
*Planter, S-4
Covered dish, S-5
*Vase, S-6
Pedestal vase, S-7
Pitcher vase, S-8
Planter, S-9
Cornucopia, S-10
*Vase, S-11
*Vase, S-12
Pitcher vase, S-13
Basket, S-14
Fruit bowl, S-15
Candleholder, S-16
Teapot, S-17
*Creamer, S-18
*Covered sugar, S-19
Covered casserole, S-20
*Beverage pitcher, S-21
Mug, S-22
*Ashtray, S-23

Plate 17

Woodland Design

Matte Glaze, Pre-1950 **Glossy Glaze, 1952**

Both lines have raised marks in script Hull U.S.A.

Top row: 1. and 3. Console bowls, W-19-10½". 2. Cornucopia, W-2-5½". 4. Double bud vase, W-15-8½".
Middle row: 1. Planter, W-14-10". 2. Console bowl, W-29. 3. Cornucopia, W-10-11". 4. Double bud vase, W-15-8½".
Bottom row: 1. Pitcher vase, W-6-6½". 2. and 4. Candleholders, W-30. 3. Console bowl, W-29. 5. Pitcher vase, W-6-6½".

Pieces known in the Woodland design:

*Cornucopia, W-2-5½"
Ewer, W-3-5½"
*Vase, W-4-6½"
Cornucopia, W-5-6¼"
*Pitcher, W-6-6½"
*Jardiniere, W-7-5½"
*Vase, W-8-7½"
Basket, W-9-8¾"
*Cornucopia, W-10-11"
Flowerpot, W-11-5¾"
Handing basket, W-12-7½"
*Wall vase, W-13-7½"
*Planter, W-14-10"
*Double bud vase, W-15-8½"
Lamp, no mark

Vase, W-16-8½"
Vase, W-17-7½"
Vase, W-18-10½"
*Console bowl, W-19-10½"

Basket, W-22

Pitcher vase, W-24-13½"

*Teapot, W-26
*Creamer, W-27
*Sugar, W-28
*Console bowl, W-29
*Candleholder, W-30
Flowerpot, W-31-5¾"

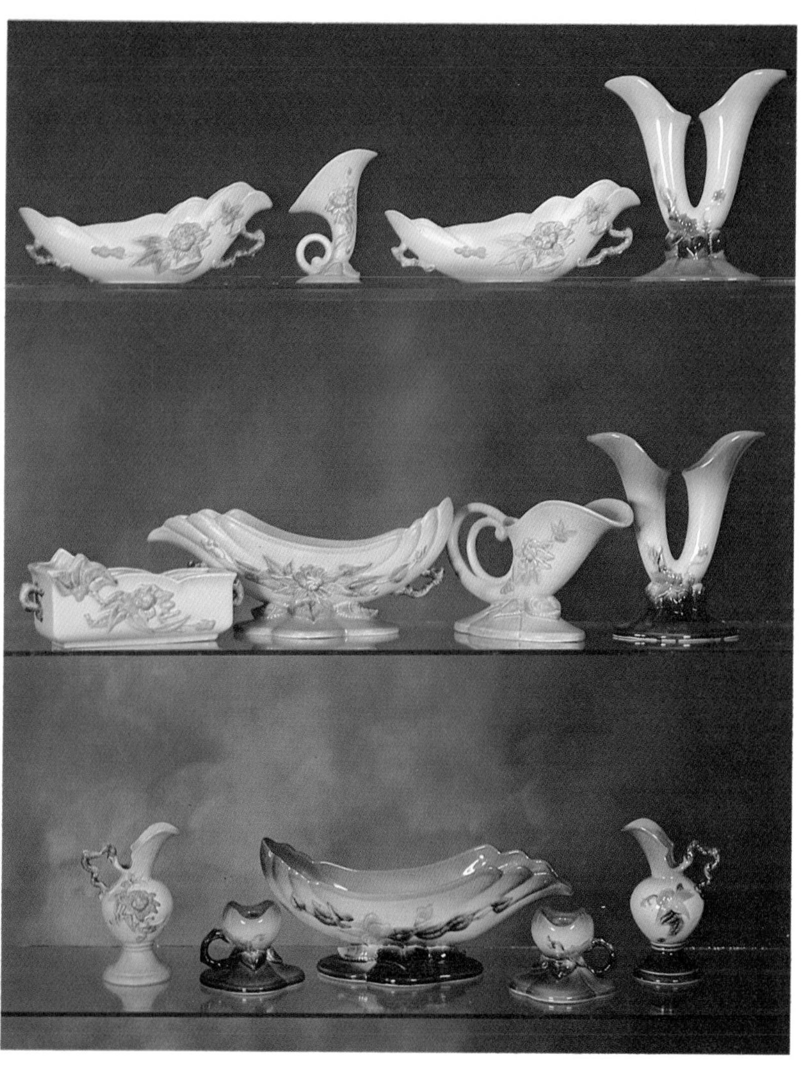

Plate 18

woodland design (continued)

Top row: 1. Lamp, no mark. 2. Wall vase, W-13-7½". 3. and 4. Covered sugars, W-28. 5. Teapot, W-26. 6. Creamer, W-27.

Middle row: 1. Jardiniere, W-7-5½". 2. Vase, W-4-6½". 3. Wall vase, W-13-7½". 4. Cornucopia, W-2-5½". 5. Vase, W-8-7½".

Bottom row: 1. Cornucopia, W-2-5½". 2. Vase, impressed HULL-URN-VASE 420. 3. Cat and spool-of-thread planter, impressed Hull (script) U.S.A. 89. 5. Combination console bowl and candleholder, impressed script Hull U.S.A. 91.

Tropicana Design

I don't have an example of this line. Its date of production is uncertain, but it is thought to be in the 1950s. It portrays Caribbean people on a white background. There are seven known pieces:

Console, T-51
Ashtray, T-52
Vase, T-53-8½"
Vase, T-54-12½"
Basket, T-55
Pitcher vase, T-56
Vase, T-57-14½"

Plate 19

Narcissus Design

This line is matte finished with block letters HULL U.S.A. impressed.

Top row: 1. Jardiniere, 413-9". 2. Jardiniere, 413-5½". 3. Vase, 404-8½". 4. Vase, 405-8½". 5. Vase, 405-7".

Middle row: 1. and 2. Vases, 403-7". 3. Vase, 403-10½". 4. Vase, 405-4¾". 5. Vase, 402-7".

Continental Design, 1959

These pieces are impressed Hull (script) U.S.A. They have a glossy finish and came in three colors, blue, persimmon, and green.

Bottom row: 1. Vase, 54. 2. Console bowl, 51. 3. Pitcher vase, 56. 4. Strawberry design vase, impressed Hull (script) U.S.A. 45. 5. Strawberry design vase, impressed Hull (script) U.S.A. 46.

Known Narcissus pieces: (many of the number series came in different sizes).

Pitcher, 401-5"
*Vase, 402-7"
*Vase, 403-10½"
*Vase, 403-7"
Vase, 403-4¾"
*Vase, 404-8½"
*Vase, 405-4¾"
*Vase, 405-7"
Vase, 405-10½"
Vase, 406-4¾"
Vase, 407-4¾"
Basket, 408-7"
Vase, 409-12"
Vase, 410-7½"
Hanging basket, 412-7"
Hanging basket, 412-4"
*Jardiniere, 413-9"
*Jardiniere, 413-5½"
Vase, 414-10½"

Known pieces from the Continental line:

Ashtray, 1
Ashtray, 3
Ashtray and penholder, 20
Ashtray and penholder, 40
*Console bowl, 51
Ashtray, 52
Vase, 53
*Vase, 54-12½"
Basket, 55
*Pitcher vase, 56
Vase, 57-14½"
Vase, 58-13¾"
Vase, 59-15"
Vase, 60-15"
Candleholder vase, 61
Covered compote, 62
Leaf dish, 63
Vase, 64
Bud vase, 66
Planter/candleholder, 67
Planter, 68
Planter, 69
Console bowl, 70
Vase, 28
Vase, 29

Plate 20

Orchid Design, 1940-41

This design has the matte glaze and is impressed in block letters HULL U.S.A.

Top row: 1. and 2. Bud vases, 306-6¾". 3. Console bowl, 314-13". 4. Vase, 309-8". 5. Vase, 304-8¾".

Middle row: 1. Bowl, can't read mark. 2. Vase, 307-6½". 3. Vase, 302-4½". Capri design, 1961—This design comes in a sea green and coral colors. It is matte finished and impressed Hull (script) U.S.A. 4. Lion head vase, 50. 5. Vase, 15.

Bottom row: These items are all impressed Hull (script) U.S.A. 1. Vase, 150. 2. and 3. Covered candy dishes, 158. 4. Basket, 56. 5. Basket, 72. 6. Basket, 56.

Known pieces in the Orchard line: (many of the number series came in different sizes).

Vase, 300-6½"
Vase, 301-4¾"
*Vase, 302-4½"
Vase, 302-10½"
Vase, 303-4¾"
Vase, 304-4½"
Vase, 304-6"
*Vase, 304-8¾"
Basket, 305-7"
*Vase, 306-6¾"
Vase, 307-4¾"
*Vase, 307-6½"
Vase, 308-4¾"
*Vase, 309-8"
Vase, 310-4¾"

*Console bowl, 314-13"
Candleholder, 315
Bookends, 316-7"x6"

Known Capri pieces:

Vase, 14
*Vase, 15
Small swan planter, 21
Large swan planter, 23
Vase, 28
Vase, 29-12"
Small basket, 38
Bowl, 44
Ribbed bowl, 45
Scalloped bowl, 46

Covered bowl, 47
Leaf basket, 48
Small lion vase, 49
*Large lion vase, 50

Ashtray, 52
Vase, 57-14½"
Vase, 58-13¾"
Vase, 59-15"
Covered compote, 62
Leaf dish, 63

Vase, 64-10"
Planter/candleholder, 67
Console/planter, 68
Llama planter, 80
Swan planter, 81
Pitcher, 87
Flying duck planter, 314
Pitcher, 525

Plate 21

Butterfly Design, 1956

These pieces have a textured finish and are impressed script Hull U.S.A. © '56.

Top row: 1. Lavabo planter, B-24. 2. Bowl, no mark. 3. Three-compartment dish, B-23. 4. Ashtray, B-3.

Middle row: 1. Compote, B-6. 2. Pitcher vase, B-15. Blossom Flite Design, 1955—These items have a glossy finish and are impressed in script Hull U.S.A. © '55. Besides the color shown here it was available in charcoal gray with pink, blue, and metallic green. 3. Covered sugar, T-16. 4. Teapot, T-14. 5. Creamer, T-15. 6. Basket, T-2.

Bottom row: 1. Vase, T-7. 2. Honey jug, T-1. 3. and 5. Candleholders, T-11. 4. Console bowl, T-10. 6. Pitcher vase, T-13.

Known pieces in the Blossom Flite line:

*Honey jug, T-1
*Basket, T-2
Pitcher, T-3
Basket, T-4

Cornucopia, T-6
*Vase, T-7
Basket, T-8
Basket, T-9-10"
*Console bowl, T-10
*Candleholder, T-11
Wine server or planter, T-12
*Pitcher vase, T-13
*Teapot, T-14
*Creamer, T-15
*Covered sugar, T-16

Known pieces of the Butterfly design:

*Ashtray, B-3

*Candy dish, B-6

Three-legged vase, B-9

Two-legged vase, B-12

*Pitcher vase, B-15

Pitcher vase, B-18

Console bowl, B-21
Candleholder, B-22
*Compartment dish, B-23
*Lavabo planter, B-24

Plate 22

Speckled Design

Most of the items on this page are marked with script Hull U.S.A. impressed. Different markings will be noted.

Top row: 1. Basket, W-9-8¾". 2. Urn, URN NO. 775-7". 3. Double fish planter (E-2 shape), no mark. 4. Urn, URN NO. 75-6". 5. Wall vase, W-13-7½".

Middle row: 1. Fish vase, (E-7 shape), no mark. 2. Compote, 65. 3. Wall vase, W-13-7½". 4. Lavabo planter, B-24.

Bottom row: 1. Dancing girl planter, 955 U.S.A. impressed. This also has the original Hull seal. 2. Pitcher wall vase, no Hull mark, impressed U.S.A. 81. 3. Vase, 110. 4. Clock planter, impressed U.S.A. 530, only. 5. Basket, impressed U.S.A. 84, only. 6. Vase, impressed U.S.A. 6½-92.

Plate 23

Stoneware

Top row: This set of a pitcher, six mugs, and covered pretzel jar is made of stoneware. It has the Ⓗ mark on all pieces. Each piece depicts people sitting around a table with a mountain scene in the background. The other side shows an Alpine-style house with pine trees and mountains in the background. The mugs are 6¼" tall, with a 3" diameter. The pitcher is 9 3/8" tall with the base diameter of 5¾". The covered jar is 9½" tall with a diameter of 6 7/8".

Middle row: 1. and 2. Vases, stoneware, $\overset{32}{\underset{8}{Ⓗ}}$ impressed. 3. Vase, stoneware, impressed $\overset{26}{Ⓗ}$. 4. Vase, stoneware, $\overset{40}{\underset{7}{Ⓗ}}$. 5. Thistle design vase, 1940-41, impressed U.S.A. 62-6½", only.

Bottom row: 1. Basket, impressed Hull (script) 44. 2. Lamb planter, impressed Hull Art U.S.A. 965. 3. Rooster planter, impressed Hull (script) U.S.A. 53. 4. Colt planter, impressed Hull (script) U.S.A. only.